Centerfield Ballhawk

by Matt Christopher

Illustrated by Ellen Beier

 HOUGHTON MIFFLIN

Boston • Atlanta • Dallas • Geneva, Illinois • Palo Alto • Princeton

Printed in Hong Kong

ISBN-13: 978-0-395-77921-7
ISBN-10: 0-395-77921-9

ISBN-13: 978-0-618-93314-3
ISBN-10: 0-618-93314-X

1 2 3 4 5 6 7 8 9   SDP   15 14 13 12 11 10 09 08

For Matthew Alexander Lurie

1

CRACK!

Crash.

The first sound came when José Mendez's bat hit the ball. The second came when the ball smashed through a car's window.

José froze.

"Oh, no!" Sparrow Fisher moaned.

"Oh, yes," José murmured, sick to the bone. The hole was baseball size, surrounded by thin zigzag cracks. It was in the left front window of Mrs. Dooley's new car. Mrs. Dooley was

José's neighbor, and she hated baseball more than crabgrass.

"Go after it, Sparrow!" José cried. "Maybe the door's unlocked!"

"Oh, yeah? *You* go after it," Sparrow said. He was ten, a year older than José, with hair the color of ripened wheat.

José clamped his jaws tight, then dropped his bat and ran across the yard to Mrs. Dooley's car. He had to jump over the hedge to get to it, but that was no problem.

The problem was the car door. It was locked. So was the rear door.

"José Mendez! Just what do you think you're doing?" a shrill voice cried out.

For the second time in twenty seconds, José froze. Mrs. Dooley, a small, skinny woman, was standing in her doorway, staring at him through her narrow glasses.

"I — I was trying to get our ball, Mrs. Dooley," José answered nervously.

She came trotting down the steps, her

slippers slapping against her feet. "What happened here? Oh, no!" she cried. "You broke a window in my car, didn't you? You'll pay for this, young man! You hear me? You'll pay for this!"

She gave José a glare that would have curled a flower, then turned back to the hole in the car window. "I knew something like this would happen," she said angrily. "You should know better than to play baseball in your front yard. Hasn't your father —"

"Yes, Mrs. Dooley," José interrupted. "My father has warned me not to. I'm sorry."

He heard footsteps behind him, and turned. His father had come out onto the porch.

"Don't worry, Mrs. Dooley," he said, his voice calm. "José will pay for it. You can bet on that."

Then his eyes bored into José's, and for the first time in his life José wished he could make himself disappear.

✻ ✻ ✻

"You are grounded from playing baseball for two weeks," José's father said to him in the house. "If the Peach Street Mudders can't get along without you for that long, too bad. I've warned you about playing pepper out there. All it takes is one hard swing and — pow! — the ball is in Mrs. Dooley's yard. This time it was worse — it hit her new car."

"I'm sorry, Dad," José said, lowering his head. "I — I didn't mean . . ." He couldn't say any more. He had no excuse. He should have known better.

José loved playing baseball so much that he tended to forget about other things. Like his father's warning.

Don't you remember what it was like, Dad? José wanted to say to him. Mr. Mendez had played in the minor league, and he had taught José everything he knew about the sport. Baseball had always been their common bond. Lately, though, things had changed. Most of the time, it seemed to José, his father was

5

angry with him. Today he had good reason to be. As for the other times, José could only conclude that he was a disappointment to his father.

Sorry, Dad, he thought. I'll make it up to you. I promise.

2

SMACK!

José's bat met the ball squarely in its center and drove it hard against the net. He popped the next two pitches and missed the next. He let the fourth pitch go by.

"What're you doing, old buddy?" a familiar voice piped up behind him. "Practicing to be a better hitter than your friend Barry 'Hit-Away Kid' McGee?"

José turned and saw Barry standing behind the batting cage screen. Barry was the Peach Street Mudders' left fielder.

"I'll never be as good as you," José said. "You're the best, Barry."

The red-headed kid with Barry grinned. Bus Mercer was the Peach Street Mudders' shortstop. "Want me to pinch-hit for you, José?" he said, kidding.

"*Somebody* might have to," José said.

He swung at the remaining pitches that shot out of the ball gun — hitting some, missing some — then stepped out of the batting cage. He wiped his sweating forehead with his shirtsleeve.

"You guys want to see a real hitter?" Bus said. "Stick around."

He paid for a round and hit every pitch but two.

Then Barry took his turn. *POW! POW! POW!*

He hit every pitch solidly. José watched him with envy. If I could hit like that, I wouldn't have to come to this batting cage, he thought. I wouldn't have to worry about being a disappointment to my father.

When the pitches stopped coming, Barry stepped out of the cage. He hadn't even worked up a sweat, José noticed.

"What *are* you doing here?" Barry asked him. "Weren't you grounded?"

"Yeah," Bus joined in. "Sparrow told us how you creamed that old lady's car."

José's face turned red with embarrassment. "I was grounded from playing on the team. My dad didn't say anything about practicing. And I figured I should stay in shape." He didn't want to tell them the real reason he was practicing. He didn't think they'd understand.

"Good idea," said Barry. "I sure hope your dad changes his mind. We really need you."

José blushed again, this time with pleasure. "Aw, I bet you won't even notice I'm not there," he said modestly.

"Sure we will," said Bus. "You're the best fielder we have."

José enjoyed the compliment, but he wished

he was valued for being a good hitter. A good hitter like his father was — he'd batted .375 when he'd played in the minors. If he could match his father's average, José figured, he might get back into his father's good graces.

With new determination, José bought another round. It was only a dollar for fourteen pitches. He stepped in the box, held his bat ready, and triggered the gun. A ball shot out of the mouth of the pitching machine like a white meteor.

José swung. *Crack!* The ball bounced off the top of his bat and hit his cheek.

Oh, no! his mind screamed as he stepped out of the batter's box and rubbed his fingers lightly over the bruise. He could feel it beginning to swell.

Yikes! How was he going to explain this to his father? He had told him that he was going over to Barry's house. A lot of good this practice session had done him!

3

The three boys quit playing and headed for home. Barry and Bus talked about the Bay Street Stingers, the team they were playing against tomorrow. José worried about the red spot on his cheek and what he'd say to his father.

When he reached his house, José saw that the garage door was open. His father was working on the car.

José walked on the grass on his way to the front porch, hoping it would muffle his footsteps.

"José?"

José stopped dead. His father had heard him.

Nervous, José turned and entered the garage. He covered the bruise with his hand, moving his fingers a little as if he were scratching an itch.

Mr. Mendez was pouring oil into the engine's crankcase. He looked at José. "You look sweaty," he observed. "You and Barry been playing ball?"

José shrugged. "Well, yeah. In a way."

Mr. Mendez's eyes narrowed. "In a way? What do you mean?"

"We were having batting practice."

His father frowned. "Batting practice? Even though I told you you were grounded?"

"From everything? I wasn't playing with the team . . ."

Mr. Mendez straightened up. He was staring at José's cheek. Suddenly José realized that he had forgotten about the bruise and had taken his hand off it.

"What happened to your cheek?" Mr. Mendez asked.

Jose's throat ached. He had to tell his father the whole truth now. "I bruised it," he said.

"How?"

"I was at the batting cage, and I fouled off a pitch."

"I see," said his father. "So you didn't go to Barry's house. You went to the batting cage instead."

José clamped his mouth shut and nodded. Out of the frying pan and into the fire, he thought.

"Why did you go to the batting cage? You've never gone there before, have you? Isn't it expensive?"

"No. It's only a buck for fourteen pitches. I've saved a few dollars from raking leaves," José explained. "And I — I wanted to work on my batting."

"I don't see why," said Mr. Mendez. "You're not going to be playing ball for a while.

14

Remember? Now, go inside. When I'm done out here, we're going to have a little talk."

José knew what that meant. His father would do all of the talking. Loud, angry talking. The ache in his throat got worse. "Yes, sir."

He started out of the garage.

"I'm disappointed, José," his father said sternly. "You tell me one thing and do something else. What's with you? Can't I trust you anymore?"

Sure, you can, Dad, José wanted to say. You just have to give me a chance.

José took a deep breath, then exhaled. "I'm sorry, Dad," he said softly.

"That's all I've been hearing from you lately: 'I'm sorry.' It's time that you took responsibility for your actions," said Mr. Mendez. "Did you call your coach yet? Tell him you won't be playing for the next two weeks?"

"No," said José. He'd been hoping, like

15

Barry, that his father would change his mind.

"You'd better," said Mr. Mendez. "Then go to your room until I call you." He turned and went back to pouring oil into his crankcase, and José went into the house to wait for another lecture.

4

Fighting back tears, José put an ice cube on his bruised cheek, then went to his room. He lay on his bed, wondering why things had gone sour with his father. Two weeks without baseball! He might as well have said two months.

If only I could make him proud of me again, José thought. Hitting .375 would do it. But how could he become a good hitter when he was one hundred percent grounded?

José groaned and punched his pillow. Then he had an idea. He could still *read* about baseball, couldn't he? Maybe he'd pick up a few pointers. José got up and looked for his book on Little League baseball.

But it wasn't on the shelf. It was missing.

He looked up, down, and sideways for the book but couldn't find it.

Somebody stole it, he thought. But who'd do that?

It had to have been Carmen. He knocked on her door and asked her about it.

"Yeah, I borrowed it," his sister replied. She was eleven, a spitting image of their mother, who had died two years earlier.

José stared at her. "What do you want it for?"

"I wanted to bone up on the rules for softball. Linda Baker is putting a team together in the girls' softball league, and she asked me to play first base!"

"That's great," José said without much enthusiasm. Maybe you'll wind up a better ballplayer than me, he wanted to add.

"What's with you?" Carmen asked, noting his glum expression. "Did you break another window?"

José scowled at her. "No, one was enough. Dad grounded me from baseball."

"Yeah, I know." Carmen shook her head in sympathy. "Maybe he'll forget about it."

"Not this time," said José. "I'm in deep."

Carmen didn't say anything for a moment. What could she say? José thought. She never had any problems with Dad.

Then she went over to her desk and pulled his book out from under a pile of homework. "Here," she said, handing it to him. "If you can't play baseball, you might as well read about it."

José smiled weakly. "Just what I was thinking," he said. "Thanks."

He left her room and picked up the phone in the hallway. He called Coach Russ Parker and told him that he couldn't play for the next two weeks.

"Why not?" Coach Parker wanted to know.

José explained, then hung up. I just hope I still remember how to play when the two weeks are up, he thought.

The team welcomed him back like an old friend two weeks later when the Peach Street Mudders played the Bay Street Stingers. During the time he'd been grounded, they had lost two games and won two. And the Stingers were living up to their name. They were like angry hornets.

But despite the Stingers' reputation, Mudders pitcher Sparrow Fisher mowed down their lead-off batter, Nick Long, with a strikeout.

Then Henry Shaw came up and blasted the first pitch to deep center field.

José turned and bolted back toward the fence. The ball was arcing down over his head. He reached out . . . far out . . .

5

The ball hit the webbing of José's glove and stuck there! It looked like a scoop of vanilla ice cream perched on a cone as José stared at it in disbelief.

He turned and whipped the ball in, his ears ringing with the joyous yell of the fans.

"Good catch, man!" Barry cried. "I didn't think you'd make it!"

"Just lucky," José said.

Ted Shoemaker grounded out to third, and the top of the first half was over.

Coach Parker and the rest of the guys greeted him warmly as he ran in to the dugout. But he thought: I hope I do as well at the plate. That was where his playing counted the most.

Barry led off with a walk, Turtleneck Jones struck out, and José stepped into the batting box. He took two balls and a strike, then leaned into one that sailed out to deep left. It was too high. He knew before he'd taken a half a dozen steps that it would be caught.

It was. Two out.

"That's okay, old buddy!" Barry said as José trotted across the infield toward the dugout. "That was close to being a round-tripper!"

But it wasn't, José wanted to say. Well, he still had two or three more bats to go.

T.V. Adams, the next batter, tripled to deep right, bringing Barry home and putting them on the scoreboard. Then Lefty Burk, the Stingers' skinny hurler, threw a wild pitch over Bus Mercer's head, and T.V. trotted in for the

Mudders' second run. Bus flied out, leaving the score Bay Street Stingers 0, Peach Street Mudders 2.

Russ Coon, the Stingers' fourth and best hitter, led off with a clothesline drive over second base that brought the Stingers' fans to their feet. The second José saw it coming, he sprang forward. He ran hard, dove on his stomach, and caught the ball just before it hit the ground.

Once again the fans cheered him.

"Terrific catch, old buddy!" Barry yelled.

Grinning, José got up, tossed the ball to him, and brushed off his uniform.

Jack Taylor singled, but first base was as far as he got. The Mudders' defense closed the top half of the inning with no runs.

Catcher Rudy Calhoun tapped the plate with his bat a few times, then singled on the first pitch for the Mudders. Nicky Chong hit into a double play.

The Mudders got another chance to score

when Alfie Maples walked. But Sparrow struck out to end the bottom of the second inning.

Jay Mancuso started off the top of the third with a single. Lefty Burk surprised the crowd by knocking a triple against the right field fence, scoring Jay, and that was the beginning of a hitting spree that ended with Russ Coon's home run over the left field fence. The half-inning ended with the Stingers on top, 4 to 2.

Holy moly! José thought dismally as he came running in from the outfield. If there was ever a time for me to get a solid hit, this is it!

Barry and Turtleneck both got on with singles. Maybe we'll start rolling now, José thought as he stepped to the plate.

"Keep it going, José!" Barry shouted.

José swung at two pitches, missed them both, and stepped out of the box. He was sweating, and his heart was beating like a drum.

6

"Ball!" boomed the ump.

"Ball two!"

Then "Ball three!" and once again, José stepped out of the batting box. He could hear Barry shouting to him from first base. "Over the fence, José!"

José took a deep breath, let it out, and stepped back in the box.

The pitch came in. He swung. *Whiff!* He'd struck out!

Sick and embarrassed, he went back to the bench. How am I ever going to hit .375 by striking out? he thought. If I do that again, Coach Parker might bench me. How can I improve by sitting on the bench? Good thing Dad isn't here to see *this*.

T.V. Adams came through with a long triple to left center field, scoring both Barry and Turtleneck, and tying the score, 4 to 4.

The Mudders' infield played some strong defense in the top of the fourth inning. Not a Stinger reached first base.

José sat glumly in the dugout as he watched Alfie step to the plate in the bottom half of the fourth. Alfie took two pitches, then flied out to left.

Sparrow got on when he drove one to center field and Hogie Mitchell, the Stingers' centerfielder, dropped it.

"All riiiight!" José cried. "Come on, Barry! Get on!"

Barry doubled to right center, sending Sparrow all around to third.

José's heart pounded as he got his bat and knelt in the on-deck circle. This was his third chance to bat. If Turtleneck didn't knock in at least one run, it would be up to him.

Turtleneck flied out.

José groaned softly as he got off his knee and went to the plate. He'd better hit, he told himself, or expect to warm the pines the rest of the game.

He powdered the first pitch. It went high and deep to center field, and for a moment he felt good. That ball was going over the fence.

It didn't. It was too high and not out far enough. Hogie Mitchell caught it just inside the fence.

José could hear the Mudders' fans moan as he hopped over the first base bag, turned, and headed back to the dugout for his glove. He waited for Coach Parker's voice, telling him to cool it for the next two innings. Instead, Coach Parker had Tootsie Malone take Alfie's place in right field and Jack Livingston take Bus Mercer's place at shortstop.

Lefty Burk singled to start off the top of the fifth. Then Nick Long popped up to third, and Henry Shaw grounded out to second, almost hitting into a double play.

"Play deep, José," T.V. said as Ted Shoemaker stepped to the plate. "This guy's got power."

Sometimes T.V. suggested where the guys should play a batter, and he was usually right. This time he was neither right nor wrong. Ted Shoemaker walked.

"Don't have to tell me about this guy, T.V.!" José yelled as Russ Coon stepped to the plate. He'd gotten a home run his last time up.

This time Russ swung at the first pitch and drove it a mile high and almost a mile deep. It was going over José's head.

José ran back . . . back . . .

7

The ball was dropping several feet behind José. He ran harder, stretched out his glove — *and caught it.*

The Mudders fans cheered, clapped, and whistled.

"Beautiful catch, José," Coach Parker praised him as he came trotting in to the bench. "Just beautiful."

"Thanks," José murmured.

"Show-off," Barry said, grinning.

José laughed.

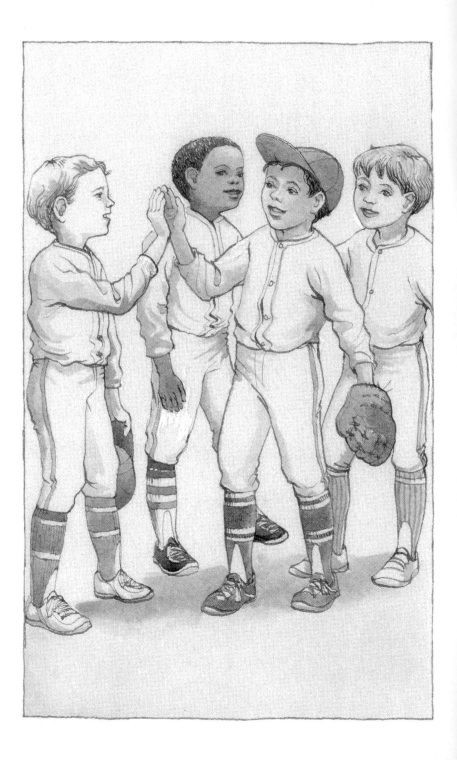

The whole team gave him high fives before he could sit down. He smiled. He hadn't felt so good in a long time.

But it was at bat where he wanted to pull off the big play. His father would want to see him hit better than anyone else.

T.V. led off the bottom of the fifth with a single, and scored on Rudy Calhoun's long double to left center field. That was all the Mudders could do that half-inning, but the run put them in the lead, 5 to 4.

"Hey, can you believe it?" Barry said as he and José ran out to the outfield together. "We're leading the champs!"

José shrugged. "Yeah, but remember the saying, 'It ain't over till it's over'?"

"Right. Yogi Berra!"

José laughed.

Jack Taylor led off the top of the last inning for the Stingers and socked the second pitch to deep left. Barry ran back and stood against the fence, watching the ball sail over his head for a home run.

Oh, man! José thought. A tied-up game! Yogi was right, he mused. Maybe — just maybe — they'll go on to win it.

Hogie Mitchell smashed out a double, and José felt that his intuition was right. Then Frankie Newhouse flied out, and Sparrow mowed the next two down with strikeouts. José breathed easier. Now it was 5 to 5.

"You're up, Sparrow!" James Boles, the Mudders' scorekeeper cried. "Break the tie! Win your own ball game, kid!"

Sparrow popped out.

Then Barry singled to left, Turtleneck popped a single over second base, and José came to bat.

"Do it now, José!" Barry yelled at first, clapping his hands. "Drive it to San Francisco!"

José took three pitches, two balls, and a

strike, then belted it. The hit was one of the longest he had ever made. It sailed over the left field fence for a home run, winning the game, 8 to 5.

José rounded the bases, listening to the whoops and applause of the Mudders' fans. I sure wish Dad could have seen that hit, he thought, even though it was the only one I made today. Maybe it would have made up for my other foul-ups at bat.

He was happy that his homer had led the Mudders to victory, but it didn't boost his average up any higher than if he had gotten a single. One hit out of four times at bat was only .250. That was a long way from .375. How he was ever going to reach that average?

It was two days later, while he was riding his bike down Main Street, that he spotted a bat in the window of Al's Secondhand Shop. Suddenly he had an idea.

Maybe a new bat could help him reach .375!

Excited, he rode up to the window and saw that the bat was the right size. Then he saw the price: eight dollars. He had saved up some money, but not that much.

He took out his wallet and counted the money he had in it. Four dollars and twenty-eight cents. Would the shop owner hold it for him? he wondered.

He left his bike on the sidewalk and went into the shop.

"That bat in the window," he said to the owner, a short man with glasses. "I've only got about four dollars. Would you hold it for me till I get the rest of it?"

"Sure, kid," the man said. "I'll hold it for two days. No more."

José stared at him. Two days? Where was he going to get four dollars in two days?

8

I might be able to borrow the money from Dad, José thought, and pay him back later. But he didn't want to. He wanted to earn it on his own.

He wasted no time getting his father's rake and going from one house to the next on the street he lived on. "Hello," he said to each person who answered his ring. "I'm José Mendez. I'll rake your lawn if you want me to."

But after calling on six homes and getting a polite "No, thank you" from each, he became discouraged and wanted to quit.

Then he decided he'd go for ten. If he didn't get a "Yes, thank you" by then, that was it. He wouldn't even ask his father for the money. He'd forfeit the four dollars he'd given to the shop owner — and wish he had never seen that bat.

He turned left on the next block, and his hopes faded almost instantly. Every lawn that he could see looked as if it had been raked just yesterday.

Then he walked half a block farther and spied a lawn that looked as if it needed raking badly. I should definitely get a "Yes, thank you" here, he thought hopefully.

He didn't get any reply at all. No one answered the door.

Three more to go, he thought, discouraged once again.

He got a "No, thank you" at the next house and a "No, thank you, kid. I'm sorry" from a man on a crutch at the next.

One more home to go. It would be a miracle if he were hired there. He might as well kiss that bat good-bye.

He was just about ready to knock on the door when he heard a shout. "Hey, kid! Come back here!"

He whirled. It was the man with the crutch. He was motioning to José.

José's heart leaped. Had the guy changed his mind? He raced back across the lawn and paused in front of the stoop.

"Yes, sir?" he said, breathing hard.

The man smiled. "I've changed my mind. I've sprained my ankle, and I don't know when I'll be able to rake my lawn. Or even mow it. What's your rate?"

"Four dollars, sir."

"Fair enough," the man said.

José took half an hour to rake the lawn. The man gave him a five-dollar bill and told him to keep the change. José's eyes shone like stars as he pocketed the money.

On his way home with the rake, José passed

Mrs. Dooley's house. Her car was parked in the street, hidden from her house by a row of hedges. He noticed a gleaming new window in place of the one he had broken, and he stopped. Even though he had paid for the damages himself, he still felt bad for the trouble he had caused Mrs. Dooley. Looking at the shining glass gave José an idea.

He quickly ran to his garage and replaced the rake. Then he hunted around in his father's car supplies until he found what he was looking for — a couple of old rags and a can of car wax. After carefully reading the directions twice, he hurried back to Mrs. Dooley's car.

A few hours later, he stood back and surveyed his work. Mrs. Dooley's car shone like new! José picked up the dirty rags and walked back to his house, tired but happy.

While he was putting the car wax away, he glanced at his watch. If he hurried, he could still make it to Al's Secondhand Shop. He grabbed his bike and sped off.

José reached the shop just before it closed. He paid the four-dollar balance due on the bat and walked out with it slung over his shoulder. When he got outside, he took a few practice swings. The bat felt just right. José could almost hear the solid crack of the bat meeting the baseball. He was sure he had the answer to his hitting problem in his hands.

But I should practice hitting with it for real, he thought. He still had a dollar left from raking — just enough for fourteen balls at the batting cage.

As he headed toward the cage, he heard the *whack! whack!* of balls being hit. He paused and looked to see who was doing the hitting.

It was Carmen, and from the number of baseballs in the net in front of her, he could tell she had been there for a while. As he stood there, he watched her make contact with nearly every ball that was pitched to her.

He couldn't believe it! Then he remembered what she had said about boning up on softball. From the looks of things, she had either done a lot of reading or inherited their dad's hitting ability.

Okay, bat, José thought, swinging one more time. Now it's *our* turn to shine!

Two minutes later, he was batting in another cage.

Crack! Crack! Crack! He hit the balls against the net just as fast and hard as they shot out of the pitching gun.

Then there was another *crack!* But this time it wasn't the bat hitting the ball.

It was the bat breaking in two.

9

"Don't feel so bad. It's just a bat," Carmen said as she rode her bike alongside José on their way home.

"Sure, it is," he said. "But it felt perfect. Did you see how I was hitting that ball? Like . . . like a big leaguer."

He wanted to say "like Dad used to hit 'em." But he didn't want her to know why he was so anxious to be a good hitter. A *real* good hitter. She'd probably laugh in his face. He would *never* be as good a hitter as their father used to be, she might say.

José and Carmen stowed their bikes in the garage and walked across the lawn to the house. Warm smells of spaghetti sauce greeted them as they entered the kitchen. Suddenly José slapped his forehead.

"Tonight's my night to fix the salad and set the table for dinner! Oh, man, how could I forget?" he cried.

"I was just wondering the same thing," said his father, walking in from the dining room. He noted their grubby appearances, shook his head, and said curtly, "Looks like I'll have to do it. You two get washed up before we eat. Dinner in fifteen minutes."

José and Carmen hurried to the bathroom and soaped their hands and faces. Carmen smiled encouragingly at him in the mirror.

"Don't worry about Dad. Just tell him you were at the batting cage. He seemed pleased when I asked if I could go there to practice," she said.

"Maybe," José replied glumly. He remembered his father's reaction the last time. Even though he wasn't grounded now, his father might be angry he hadn't asked permission to go, as Carmen had.

When they sat down to dinner, their father turned to Carmen and asked, "So, how'd my little slugger do at the cage? Your softball coach tells me you've sent the ball over the fence at least a dozen times so far. I'm impressed. We'll have to catch one of her games, won't we, José?" He ruffled Carmen's hair and smiled.

José nodded stiffly and concentrated on twirling his spaghetti onto his fork. He listened in silence as Carmen described her last homer. He was glad she was playing so well, but the sudden lump in his throat made it difficult for him to swallow the forkful of spaghetti.

I've *got* to start hitting better, he thought fiercely. I've just got to.

*   *   *

Tuesday was perfect baseball weather. The sun was shining brightly, it was hot, and there was just enough breeze to make it comfortable.

The Peach Street Mudders were playing the Stockade Bulls, a team that averaged at least six runs a game. With his new bat broken in two, José had little hope that he would raise his batting average to anywhere near .375. He would never gain back the respect he wanted so badly from his father.

The Mudders batted first. Barry led off with a double, and Turtleneck popped out, bringing up José. Okay, José thought, tapping the plate with the end of his bat. I've got to start off with a hit. I might be up only two more times. Three, if I'm lucky.

He waited until he got a two-and-two count, then walloped Eddie Mosk's knee-high pitch to deep right field. His heart leaped for a moment. *Go over. Go over,* his mind screamed.

Phil Koline caught it about ten feet in from the fence. Two out. José sighed as he saw his chances of even hitting .333 getting slimmer.

T.V. Adams, batting fourth, singled through short, scoring Barry. Then Bus struck out, ending the top of the first inning.

"You really laid into that one, José!" Barry yelled as he and José ran out to their positions. "I thought sure it was going over!"

"But it didn't," José said, disappointed.

The Stockade Bulls started off strong their turn at bat. The first two guys singled. Then, with two out, Chet Barker doubled, scoring both runs.

"Bear down, Sparrow!" T.V. Adams shouted from third.

"Not too easy on those guys, Sparrow!" José yelled from center field.

Eddie Mosk grounded out.

"Let's go!" Coach Parker cried as he headed for the third-base coaching box. "Give 'em all you've got, Rudy!"

Rudy flied out. Nicky Chong singled, then got out on Alfie's double-play hit to shortstop. It was a fast half-inning. Mudders 1, Bulls 2.

Not until the third inning did the Mudders begin to threaten again. Sparrow led off with a sizzling single through short, Barry walked, and Turtleneck bounced one over the second baseman's head, filling the bases.

José came up to bat, and his heart had never beat faster or harder.

The crowd was yelling, "Drive it out of the lot, José!"

He took three straight pitches, all inches away from the plate, and stepped out of the box. A walk would put him on base, but it wouldn't help his batting average. C'mon, Eddie, he thought. Give me something good to swing at.

He stepped back into the box and watched as Eddie wound up for the pitch.

10

"Steeerike!" yelled the ump.

Then, "Steeerike two!"

"Belt it, José!" cried the coach.

José's heart pounded like crazy. This was it.

Crack! His bat met the ball head-on. The white sphere took off like a rocket for left field and sailed over the fence for a home run!

The Mudders' fans screamed their heads off. "All right, José!" they shouted as he dropped his bat and trotted around the bases.

Bus singled that inning, too, but the Mudders failed to score him. Mudders 5, Bulls 2.

The Stockade Bulls came to bat blowing through their nostrils. After two outs and a man on third base, Adzie Healy lambasted one. It had a home run label on it as it zoomed toward the center field fence. José started to run back the instant he had seen it hit.

He was almost up against the fence when the ball came flying down over his head. He jumped — and caught it!

"Yes! Great catch, man!" Barry yelled. "Saved us a run!"

José smiled and tossed the ball to him as they ran in together. "Just lucky," he said.

"Sure." Barry laughed.

Alfie singled, and Turtleneck walked, bringing José up to the plate. *I've got to get a hit,* he thought. *I've got to, or I'm sunk.*

He grounded out.

Good thing Dad isn't at the game, he thought as he returned to the bench. At least he's got Carmen.

The Mudders kept the Bulls from scoring in the bottom of the fourth, then went to town at their turn at bat, scoring two runs. Mudders 7, Bulls 2.

In the bottom of the fifth, the Stockade Bulls showed the real power they had, as if they had purposely kept it hidden until now. They pounded Sparrow for five runs, tying up the score, 7 to 7.

In the top of the sixth, Barry singled, then Turtleneck flied out. José slowly stepped to the plate. This could be it, he thought. A hit now could break the tie. And it would mean a .500 average for him.

He flied out.

José's heart sank into his stomach. He wished he could vanish.

Then T.V. struck out, and the Bulls were back up to the plate.

The first two guys got on. Then Ted Jackson popped up to the pitcher, and Adzie blasted a line drive to center field. It looked as if it were going to hit the ground halfway between second base and José.

José was after it like a gazelle. He knew he had to catch that ball or the game was over.

He dove, then felt the solid *thud!* as the ball landed squarely in his glove.

The crowd stood up, and clapped and cheered for a full minute.

On the next play, a grounder skittered through T.V.'s legs. A run scored, and the game was over. The Blockade Bulls beat the Peach Street Mudders, 8 to 7.

"It's my fault we lost! My fault!" T.V. moaned as José caught up with him and they walked off the field together.

"Don't sweat it, man!" José said. "It's not the end of the world! Who's perfect?"

He was thinking of his batting as he said it. One out of four was .250. Far, far from a .375 average. His father would never, *never* think much of him as a baseball player.

Suddenly he heard his name called. "José!

Wait up!"

He turned.

"Dad!" he cried, surprised. "When did you get here?"

"At the beginning of the fourth inning," Mr. Mendez said.

José's face clouded. "Then you saw . . ." he started to say, but couldn't go on. How could he face his father when he'd gotten out three out of four times at bat?

"What do you want to say, son?" Mr. Mendez asked, putting his arm across José's shoulders.

"I wanted to make you proud of me," José blurted out. "I know I've been messing up lately, but I thought if I could hit .375, like you did when you played in the minors, I could make up for disappointing you. I — I'm sorry, Dad. I know I've let you down."

Mr. Mendez stopped short and looked down at José. "Is that why you've been so down in the mouth?" he exclaimed.

José sighed, then nodded.

"Listen, son," Mr. Mendez said, "I may be disappointed when you go against my wishes — like you did when you hit Mrs. Dooley's car — but I'm not disappointed in *you*. I trust you when you say you're sorry, and that's that. As far as Mrs. Dooley is concerned, I know you've worked hard to make it up to her. From what I hear," he added, smiling, "you even applied a little extra elbow grease to her car the other day."

José blushed.

Then Mr. Mendez took a deep breath and went on: "It's been hard since Mom died . . . on all of us. I've had to depend on you and Carmen to pull your own weight . . . maybe too much." He grinned. "I seem to have forgotten how hard it can be to concentrate on anything when it's baseball season. Maybe we both need to be more aware of what the other person is feeling. I'll try, if you will."

José nodded happily.

56

"And one more thing. Forget about trying to hit like I did, okay? You don't have to. You're a born outfielder, José! You've made catches that I never would have been able to, not in a million years."

José stared at him. "Really? You mean you . . . don't mind that I can't hit?"

José's father chuckled. "'Can't hit?' If you call belting a grand slam homer not hitting, well, son, we've got to sit down and have a serious talk about the game of baseball! José, you're a born ballhawk, so stop worrying about the hitting and concentrate on your fielding. That's where your team needs you the most."

José couldn't believe his ears. All this time he had thought . . . But then he recalled the joyous cheers after each catch he had made that day and smiled.

"Thanks, Dad," he murmured. "I never thought about that. I just figured the guys were being nice when they said they counted

on me being in the outfield." He glanced up at his father. "I like having people depend on me, Dad."

His father squeezed his shoulder. "Come on. We'll pick up some ice cream and celebrate those catches with Carmen. I understand she's had a hard afternoon, smashing one homer after another for her team. Looks like both of you kids are a chip off the old block, eh?"

José laughed. He never felt better in his life as he walked with his father to the car.

I might never get a .375 average, he thought. But I'm a hit with my father, and that's what counts the most.